THE
PHAT-KRUSHER
Spiritual and Physical Fitness

A GUIDE FOR KIDS
TO BETTER THEIR LIVES

PHAT-KRUSHER · SQUASH FAT LIKE A JELLY BEAN ·

AL D. WORDLY, P.T.A.

The Phat-Krusher - Spiritual & Physical Fitness
A Guide for Kids to Better Their Lives

Prolific Pen Publishing Company

ISBN: 0-692-31367-2
ISBN-13: 978-0-692-31367-1

Book Cover and Interior Design: Donna Osborn Clark
www.CreationByDonna.com

IN LOVING MEMORY
OF
MY SISTER:

REMONIA RUTH WORDLY

ALPHA

OMEGA

04/27/1960

10/08/2009

FORWARD

It seems like in each generation more kids are becoming disobedient to their parents, and are falling into some lifestyle of crime. They are very young and increasingly, are becoming more overweight and obese at an early age – 6 to 13 years old.

Mainly, it is because we as the parents forgot our kid's purpose in this life and their future life to come. Growing up is a process, therefore, their spiritual and physical lives must be nourished rightfully or both lives will fail them; if we aren't careful it can even affect our lives as parents.

In this book, Al will be talking to your precious little ones about growing up spiritually and physically. As well, Al would like to talk to the children's parents – their physical instructor, on how to help your kids mature into their rightful age; along with growing with God and you (their parents).

- Carolyn J. Wordly- Smith, ARNP-BC

CONTENTS

ACKNOWLEDGMENTS

First, and foremost, I would like to give thanks to my Lord and Savior, Jesus Christ. I would also like to give thanks to everyone that has helped to make this possible and stood beside me. When I was discouraged, someone would come in my path to keep me encouraged every step of the way. One of those people being Ms. Toya Davis! Thank you for your wonderful work in helping me to succeed.

Thanks are due to my wonderful mother, Mrs. Dorothy Wordly, who has never let me go or forsaken me; my loving sisters: Doris McClendon, Carolyn Smith, Brenda Darling; my nieces' Latoya Phillips, Terrika Darling, Jacqueline McClendon; my nephew Darius McClendon; my cousin Kelsey Adams; and my oldest son's mother, Monique Harris.

Special acknowledgement to the guys who have been side by side, and inch by inch with me in the process of the long struggle; they put up with my mess when I would be stressed: Johnny Stuart, Derrick Houston, Horry Campbell, Robin Gardner, Anthony Williams, Michael Martin, and Doyle Grimes.

To my boys, Al Jr. and Devin Wordly, whom I love dearly, and I pray they will learn to understand how important it is to follow in the path of God. Also, to my daughter-in-law Woodia Jacquet Wordly, and grandson, Adyn Wordly; their support and love is always faithful.

Last but not least, I give very warm and special thanks to my readers — thank you for your support.

CHAPTER ONE

PRAY TO GOD PERSISTENTLY

Hi kids, and how are you? Or should I Say "skippers," How are you?; because all of you are captains of my ship. In my book, there are no losers. Therefore, if you think you are loser, think again! If someone has ever called you a loser, you need to tell Him or her to think again!

I believe that every person that God created has failed at something or at some point in their lives; whether it was while we were young, teenagers or adults.

Do you know what a true winner is? It's someone who has never given up! That's right, someone that may have lost, but has the inner strength to keep trying and trying, knowing in their hearts that they will one day succeed. I believe that a champion is someone who can get back up when he or she has failed at anything in life; yet isn't afraid to try again. This is what I call a true champion.

The Bible says, *"For a good person falls seven times and rises up again; but a bad person shall fall into harm."*

- Proverbs 24:16

So if you think you have failed or perhaps you think you're failing at something such as a class in school, or at your favorite sport, think again!

Don't be too hard on yourself because these are the bumps in the road that make you stronger, and builds character. And above all, never, ever, think that you are failing your parents. They love you, and will never see you as a failure. Remember, they have been there too.

So don't be too hard on yourself, okay? Just remember that there's always tomorrow and everything works itself out over time. Practice makes perfect! Day by day, and little by little, stay moving towards the goals that you've set for yourself. You're all my little champions!

Next, I would like to talk a little about your spiritual and physical side. Did you know that you have two lives? Well, if you did not know, let me take a moment to explain it to you. One is your physical life; which is the life you're now living with your parents. Your other life is your spiritual life, which is the life you're going to live with God and Jesus (a life after death). Youngsters remember, you do have two precious lives!

In regards to your spiritual side and Jesus Christ, who is better known as God; you may be used to saying God, others may be used to saying Jesus. But children, this I can guarantee you, that God and Jesus are one and the same, which means they are One!!!

You may have heard older people say Jesus or God; such as your mom, dad, friend or someone else? As for myself, I love to say Jesus! Do you know why? Because Jesus is the One who led us to God.

Yes! Jesus introduced us to God by dying on the cross so I could meet God. This is what I want to talk to you about – meeting God, so that you can experience more of Jesus and God for yourself.

In the Bible, did you know Jesus used you (children) as an example for us adults to follow? Jesus said, *"I thank you O Father, Lord of heaven and earth, because you have hid these things from the people who think they are wise or prudent* ("educated") *and have revealed them unto babes* (children).

-Matthew 11:25

Jesus says, *"Verily I say unto you, whosoever shall not receive the Kingdom of God as a little child shall in no wise enter therein."*

-Luke 18:17

You see, kids? Jesus said that in order for us adults to be with God, or Him (Jesus), we must be like you. With your kind of gentleness, love, faith, belief, meekness, humbleness, and trust towards God and Jesus. Why? Because you children already have these beautiful qualities within yourselves.

Wow! Doesn't this make you feel very special? To know that Jesus used you as an example for us adults to follow. Jesus loves you so much that he chose you first. The same way as when you have a bunch of toys, and your parents tell you to pick your favorite one, but there are a lot of toys around and you can only pick one. Of course you're going to pick the one that you most cherish, the very best, the one above all others, right? Well, that's the same way Jesus and God feel towards you. You are all very special to Them, no matter what.

Just always remember that Jesus loves you and you're special to Him, no matter what.

If you're not familiar with God, I want you to use this book as your compass or 'road-map' to help you become more familiar with God and Jesus.

The first step of getting to know Jesus and God is simply praying. Today everyone uses technology; we see and use computers, email, and texting as tools to communicate with each other. Yet to communicate with God and Jesus, we use prayer to talk (or) communicate with Them.

Jesus wants you to get familiar with God, and God wants you to get familiar with Jesus. Just as you would get familiar with a friend by talking to Him or her, so you can get to know them better.

God and Jesus want to have a sense of closeness with you, just like the closeness you have with your mother, dad, sister, brother, or with a friend. God and Jesus desire that same kind of closeness with you.

Do you know why God and Jesus want to have a closeness with you? Because they both love you so much. You may not be able to see Them, but I can surely tell you that their love is there for all of you.

Let me share a little secret with you. Just as your parents or guardian take care of you by protecting, providing, and loving you, as well as take care of themselves by going to work each day. My secret is that God and Jesus are the Ones who are protecting, providing for, and loving them too.

God awakens your parents or guardian to get up each morning to be able to go to their job each day, so that they are able to take care of you.

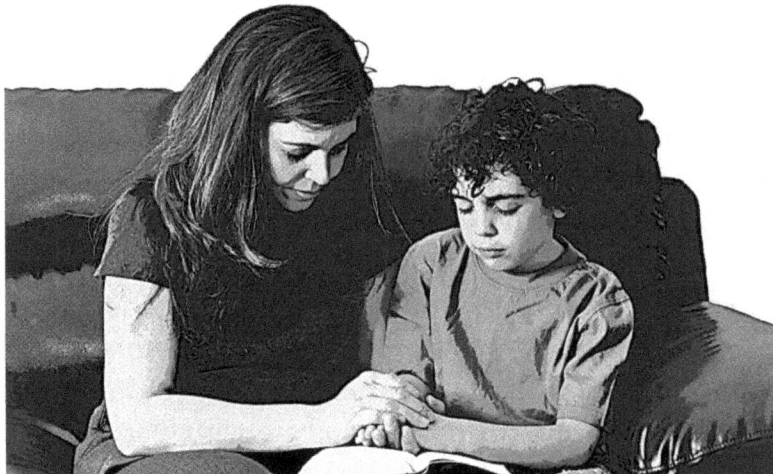

God and Jesus Protect, provide, and love us all. More plainly, he simply loves all people throughout the world. So children, the next time mom and dad, or guardian, say that they take care of you, be mindful and know our God and Jesus are there protecting, providing for, and loving them too. And that's our honest secret.

I want you to grow closer to God by praying more often. Believe it or not, God talks to us more than we think. Especially to you, children. He can talk to you as many times as you need Him to.

God loves to train children while they're very young. Therefore, you will remember Him (God), as you begin to grow up into adults. This is why God tells us as parents to bring our children up into the Lord.

The Bible says: *"Train up a child in the way he should go: and when he is old, he will not depart from it."*

-Proverbs 22:6

This is only to help you children to remember God! This will help guide and protect you in the right way to live. So that you can be a good person unto God and to your wonderful parents. Now you can begin to show some of us adults how we should act, and live!

Listen, you're at the right age to be totally awesome with God. Especially now that you know God and Jesus love you.

The Two are there, waiting to hear your precious voice each and every morning, day, and night, before you go to bed, after you wake up, or anytime you'd like. They're always listening for your voice. This is how you'll become more familiar with God and Jesus, and how they'll become more familiar with you. Simply by praying, and the more the better!

Imagine! If I was the person that was giving your parents or guardian the money to take care of you and them; with the extra money your parents or guardian could buy you a toy, or a video game ever day of every week. Whatever toy or game you wanted. Yet, you and your parents never know who

I am, and I'm always giving to you all.

Now wouldn't you want to know who I am? The person who is giving your parents the money to take care of you, and them, and of course buying you your favorite toy or game.

If my guess is right, your answer is YES! You definitely want to know who I am. Because if this were true, I would be something like a superhero to you, wouldn't I? You would be so curious to know or see who I am.

In so many more ways than one, God and Jesus are our very own Superheroes. They both have powers that we would consider supernatural, because they defy explanation. They are both very powerful in so many ways; they have the power to not have any weaknesses, and never will fail, nor can they be beaten.

Whomsoever God or Jesus fight against, they will be victorious. Their enemies will lose every time!!!

And this is why you should choose to meet them, in every way, throughout your entire life, because they're always going to be there to make sure you're awakened every single morning. Protecting, providing for and loving you unconditionally.

It's disappointing, and sad, but I must say that some adults don't want to give thanks to God and Jesus for waking them up each morning.

God and Jesus are due more credit than any person, place or living thing, which is made on the face of this earth. This is why God is trying to reach out to you children so early in your lives.

God is asking us parents or guardians to help Him in directing children straight to Him. This book will help us parents to do just that, guiding our children unto Jesus Christ our Savior, and The Father (God).

Let me show you how to do such a thing, so you can become more familiar with God and Jesus for yourselves.

Studies show that when you do a specific thing repeatedly for twenty-one days straight over and over again, it will become a lifetime habit for you.

This means that when you do something over and over again it becomes a habit, and easier for you over a period of time. This is how you form good-habits, through persistent praying unto God.

If you start praying habitually you'll form good behavior, conduct, and actions towards God, over and over again.

Just as a person learns the habit of washing their face every morning, which becomes a routine behavior, so too does praying (talking) to God become a habit, and it's a really good one.

I'm sure you've heard the old saying that practice makes perfect, it's true. If you pray in the morning and at night time, before you go to bed, you'll discover God is there for you, waiting to hear from all of you.

A child that grows up without God or Jesus in their lives will almost be certain to experience a lot of very terrible things, or become someone who won't ever find greatness. This is because he or she isn't living their life to know God and Jesus, the ones that love them the most.

But not only that, because there's another problem going on with this child. As this child grows into an adult, it will be a lot harder for them to get to know God or Jesus, maybe because of their bad behavior in life. This is why it's so important for children to get familiar with God and Jesus at an early age.

God is love! And he wants you to know His love is there for you. This is totally awesome itself. "It's always important for us as adults to protect our youth."

Now I want you to make a list of your good habits that you want to start doing. As you write them down try to focus on them; try to target each one of them day by day.

Don't try to do two or three at one time.

This way they won't be hard for you to keep up with. Try each day for twenty-one days, then, move down the list as you see progress try to master them all; ask God to help you with each task so you can achieve them all.

Now that you have written down all of your good habits, this has made God happy already. I know this will make your parents happy too!

On your list make sure you put God first. God will certainly remind you of the rest just in case you forget. He will also give you the strength to do them all.

Most importantly, you have to be very honest with yourself. Be open, honest, and willing to stay focused on your good habits.

Because good habits in life will only allow you to develop the good habits of a champion!

Here is a list that you can start off to help you on your journey to good-habits in seven steps. The number seven represents God's completion.

REMEMBER TO BE HONEST!

The Phat-Krusher list: we will call this the "**I Will**" list:

1. **I WILL**: Start praying to God more. In the morning before I go to bed and if it's possible, in the evenings too. I will make sure to pray persistently.

2. **I WILL**: Try to follow God and how He leads me.

3. **I WILL**: Try to add God in all the things I do, even while I'm performing my duties and chores around the house.

4. **I WILL**: Take on my responsibilities that my parents, guardians or teachers assign me to do.

5. **I WILL**: Not be something I am not, but be who God says I am.

6. **I WILL**: Not run from any of my problems or troubles that I will experience as I am growing up. Instead, I will face them head-on, with God, my wonderful parents, or guardian.

7. **I WILL**: Attend church more often, where I can hear God's words, and meet kids my own age that share my love for God and Jesus, along with reading the Bible to each other.

Stick this list on your bedroom door to remind you of each task as you master them. Remember! Praying can be done on your knees, sitting, standing, or even as you walk to school. God is everywhere, waiting to hear from you. God and Jesus love you, no matter what!

To parent(s):

Important! Parents remember to let your children know that you are serious about their intimacy with God; their development and growth in knowing Him better.

Also parents, in order to get your child back in the rightful place with God, we must take our place and play our roles in direction our child's attention to the one who is the best at guiding theirs', and our lives in the most magnificent way, and that's God Himself.

God created us, designed the world, and made everything on earth and heaven. Surely, he can handle our children. Therefore, as the kid's parents, we must trust God with them. This is exactly what God wants us to do… trust in Him! Due to the fact our children have special purposes in this life; God is there to make sure we can fulfill those purposes for them.

If a child grows up without the concept and values of God and the Bible, the chance of this child displaying disobedience towards their parents, guardians or authorities will be great.

This is why God is directing you and me to get our children in a good habit of knowing Him immediately.

I don't mean that you have to force God on your child, but rather, offer God to the child. We don't serve a God who teaches anything done by force, but teaches only by love.

Remember, they are your young children, so they're willing to listen to you as their instructor.

As a parent I've discovered most parents find it hard to directly show their children their own spiritual side. Why? Because all too often the parent themselves don't believe they have one.

Unfortunately, we all must pass away at some point, and meet God. This means and reveals clearly a 'LIFE' does exist and lives within us all.

The point I am making is that most parents teach and guide their children to learn about history, reading books, sports and TV shows, as well as how to use the bathroom, wash hands, clean themselves, tie shoes, dress themselves, and how to read and write at a very young age.

In it, these are good habits. Yet we know that there are parents who will also show or teach their children to use profane language do drugs, smoke cigarettes, and break the law. Some of these people we know ourselves.

However when it comes to training them up towards our Awesome God, seemingly, parents have no understanding regarding Him. This is why more of our children go astray, or end up in jails or prison!

Another point; when we look at the news, view our schools and look at America's criminal justice system, sadly we see and hear a lot of negativity.

Though Jesus says in the world there will be trouble, but it doesn't necessarily have to be your children who're causing the trouble.

The Bible teaches us to 'train up a child' in the way he or she should go, "unto the Lord." It would be in the best interest of the child, as well as for us and unto God.

We shouldn't ever rely on the world to train-up our children. Please don't raise your child that way... the world's way. Especially in this day and age; the streets and bad neighborhoods have just exactly that, a 'bad plan' for your child.

The fact of the matter, we as parents, those that follow the path of God should be teaching the world on how a child should be raised.

Therefore, begin with prayer for God's Plan, to be the plan for your children...

Believe me, you won't regret it!!!

CHAPTER TWO

BE OBIDENT TO YOUR PARENTS AND GOD

Parent(s):

Every parent desires for their kids to be obedient to them. It's why as parents we spend a great deal of our time to raise them in their youthful years.

Only because we want to direct their young lives into the best life possible that we know is favorable for them to live.

Yet, by this same token, God designed obedience unto us. Therefore, we can live the best life that God sees fit for all of us to live. Overall obedience is the way to spiritual, physical, emotional, and moral success.

God has given every one of us a series of links to the things that reflect obedience unto Him. It's very important to be obedient unto God, so that He can reveal his plan unto us.

Can you imagine a country without a president? A world without their leader, an army without a general, a child without their mother or father, a neighborhood without police officers, a church without a pastor, a school without a teacher, and a person without God?

The fact is, it would be total chaos without these positional people being in control of the matter.

However, through our obedience unto such people that are in control or have the position over us comes order. Thus, we all need to be obedient unto God. So we can all live a life of obedience unto Him. (The Awesome God!)

Your children need guidance from God and to yourself as well. We must trust and allow God to work with us in directing our children unto Him. Remember, we aren't completely capable of protecting our kids or ourselves, without God. We need the supernatural intervention of God's power.

To Kid(s): Hello Youngsters,

Now that your wonderful parents have the direction and advice to direct you through God's power, you must always remember to be obedient to them.

Obeying and honoring your parents will make them happy. When you understand how important that is, God will bless you in a special way. God even said that Himself!

In the Bible scripture, which is known as God's own written words, He explains how children must obey and honor their parents.

Don't you know? Your actions towards your parents affects God's actions towards you.

When you make your parents happy, you will make God happy too. If you really would like to make God happy, then be obedient toward your parents. Listen to the direction and good advice that your parents or guardian gives you. Honor this and God will honor you.

To honor your mother and father is one of God's Ten Commandments. We will discuss God's Ten Commandments, and as we do, feel free to try to memorize them. I have listed them below:

1. **You should have no other Gods before Me.**
2. **You should not make unto you any graven image, or any likeness of anything that is in the heaven above or in the water under the earth. You should not bow down yourself to them nor serve them.**
3. **Thou shall not take the name of the Lord in vain.**
4. **Remember the Sabbath day to keep it holy.**
5. **Honor your father and mother, that your days may be long upon the earth, which the Lord your God gives you.**
6. **You should not kill.**
7. **You should not commit adultery.**
8. **You should not steal.**
9. **You should not bear false witness against your neighbor.**
10. **You should not covet, do not want anything that belongs to someone else. Animals, house, wife, husband, etc.**

-Exodus 20:3-17

To make the commandments easy to memorize, just turn to the book of Matthew in the Bible, where Jesus said it best:

Jesus said unto them: *"You should love the Lord your God with all your heart and with all your soul, and with all your mind. And this is the first greatest commandment. And the second is like unto it; you should love your neighbor as yourself. And these two commandments hang all the Law and the Prophets."*

-Matthew 22:37-40

Kids! Do you know who your neighbor is? Well, Jesus says it's the people that show mercy unto you. You will find this passage in the book of Luke chapter 10, verses 33-37.

Jesus said these two commandments, because if a person loves God with all their heart, soul, and mind, that person wouldn't do those things in the Ten Commandments that are against God. This is the first commandment that Jesus said.

The second Commandment is just like the first. Because if a person loves someone else as much as he or she loves themselves, he or she wouldn't be doing all of the stuff that God said not to do towards someone else. This is certainly why Jesus said these two things. So that you and I will not get confused to the rules or law that are in God's Ten Commandments.

Obedience is simply doing what God or Jesus asks you to do. They are both asking you to be obedient to your parents. So you should do just that. You will make God, Jesus, and your parents happy!

God says:

"Children! Obey your parents in the Lord for this is right. To honor your father and mother, which is the first commandment, with promise; that it may be well with you and you may live long on the earth."

-Ephesians 6:1-3

"Listen unto your father that begat you and despise not your mother when she is old."
-Proverbs 23:22

Did you know that it is quite easy to impress God? You're probably asking how. All that it takes is doing exactly what he says… and you'll be doing something exactly right. (All of the time.)

So try your very best to listen to your wonderful parents. As well as those positive and good thoughts you have inside of your mind. Because that's the place where God is talking to you. This is the exact place where it's better known as the inner voice of God. So, always listen very carefully to those good thoughts and you'll achieve good things in this life.

Obedience is always rewarded by God. The blessing of God is always guaranteed to those who do right unto Him and towards their parents. It will be a True blessing to you in this life and the next life ahead.

Here is another fantastic list to add to your bedroom door. This is called:

THE PHAT KRUSHER "**NEVER WILL**" LIST

1. **Never Will** – I be disobedient to God and my parents.
2. **Never Will** – I quit school.
3. **Never Will** – I use drugs, alcohol, nor smoke.
4. **Never Will** – I use bad words to anyone, especially my parents.
5. **Never Will** – I hate anyone, but I'll try to love them just as Jesus loves me.
6. **Never Will** – I stop praying to God and reading the Bible, along with going to church.
7. **Never Will** – I say, I can't do anything, but I will try until I can do it right. I will be determined and motivated to succeed in life.

Finally! Youngsters, I need you to know one more thing! Obedience is the only real proof that you love God and your parents.

So Be O-o-Obedient!!!

To Parent(s):

Precious parents; God also left some rules for you concerning obedience; to help in the upbringing of your precious child.

The Bible says:

"And you fathers and mothers, provoke not your children to wrath; but bring them up in the nurture and admonition of the Lord."

-Ephesians 6:4

"But Jesus said suffer little children and forbid them not, to come unto me: for such is the kingdom of heaven."

-Matthew 19:14

You shouldn't be afraid or embarrassed to bring your children up unto the Lord. Just because most of the world may not do it, that doesn't mean you should neglect your child or for that matter any child from knowing God.

Surely, I recognize and know it is uncommon for a generation such as today, to be brought up in the faith of knowing Jesus Christ.

Every day you look around, we can see the results and it's all over the world. So many misguided youths and adults, senseless violence due to violent acts of misguided people. Therefore, don't let the world influence you in how you raise your children. However, you should influence the world in how your child should be raised. We certainly need God to help us in these days in which we live in.

If we practice what God says and allow our family to live according to His word, your family unit will flourish and have an abundance of blessing from God.

People often wonder why their times and days are so difficult to live in; that's only because most people tend to live a disobedient life towards an Awesome God.

Parents, you need to look out for your children's best interests by doing what God says. Give God a chance with your children; let Him usher in His best gifts unto them. But first you must teach them obedience.

TRAIN YOUR CHILDREN IN GOD'S WAY!!!

CHAPTER THREE

GOD HEARS YOUR PRAYERS AND SEES YOU TOO!

To kid(s):

Since you are getting into the habit of praying and talking to God more, you may wonder, does God really hear you? Well I can assure you that God sees you and hears your precious prayers. They truly matter to Him.

Do you know why your prayers matter to God? It is because he loves you, and he loves hearing and talking to you.

Can you imagine if you and your parents never talked to each other? The whole house would be as quiet as a mouse. And when it was time to talk and listen to each other, you would more than likely ignore each other, because of the fact you all have developed the bad behavior of not talking to each other. This will not be good, especially when something is troubling you.

That wouldn't be so good, now would it? No, it wouldn't, because you would want your parents to know what's wrong with you, so they can help or talk to you about your concerns and if possible, take the trouble and pain away.

Also, it would not feel good to your parents, if they just sat there and watched you hurt or see you in your pain; you know why? Because they love you so much. This is the same way, how God feels towards people, when they don't communicate to Him or tell Him about their pain, hurts, and troubles.

In fact, do you know? Every time a person decides not to talk to God – God hurts! …He hurts because He desires to be a part of everybody's lives! God doesn't want you kids to grow up like most of us adults, who live a life without ever knowing Him. God wants to be a part of our everyday lives. It's also important to know that it hurts God to just sit there and see people hurting and not taking their problems before Him. Even though God sees and knows people are hurting or troubled; He still wants people to invite Him into their burdens and troubles, so He can help them get through it.

God likes for us to ask Him for His help!

The Bible says:
"The eyes of the lord are upon righteous, and his ears are open unto their cry." The righteous cry, and the lord hears and delivers them out of all their troubles."
-Psalms 34:15-17

These scriptures teach us that God really cares for us, and wants us to bring our troubles to Him.

The Bible also says:

"In my distress or trouble I called upon the lord, and cried to my God: and he did hear my voice out of his temple, and my cry did enter unto his ears."

-2 Samuel 22:7

Therefore, you don't ever have to wonder or be curious about whether God hears your prayers and sees you. God Himself even said it.

There is something else I would like to share with you about prayer. I would like to begin by sharing with you a little story about a group of people in the land of Egypt.

These people are found in the book of Exodus in the bible. You may already be familiar with the story. However, if you aren't, I'm going to share the story of these people with you.

Let's begin. The people in the land of Egypt were known as slaves and were treated as slaves in the land of Egypt. They were held in captivity and imprisoned. They were held against their own will for many generations.

One day they decided to call on God with a sincere heart and asked Him to help them get out of bondage and their troubles.

The Bible says:

"And the lord said, I have surely seen the affliction (pain) of my people which are in Egypt and have heard their cry by reason of their taskmasters (burden), for I know their sorrows and I am come down (send help) to deliver them out of the hands of the Egyptians, and to bring them up out of that land unto good land and a large, unto a land flowing with milk and honey."

-Exodus 3:7-8

What I'm trying to say is…God doesn't answer every prayer right away. Some prayers, he answers fast and some God will allow some time to pass. In other words, he will answer, but it's on his time.

Like unto prayers of the people in the land of Egypt, their prayers were answered slowly, because they had to wait on the right timing of God.

Indeed, it was a very slow process, but it was right on time for "the people" who had suffered for so long in the land of Egypt.

The story tells us how our God is very merciful and he does hear our prayers. Because they finally did receive the help they were looking for. And that was to be set free from their captivity and imprisonment.

Lastly, the story tells how the people were able to witness the power of God working in their situation. God wanted them to know they are serving a real, true living God.

God was there the whole time on the scene, in front and behind the scene. This is God's way for people to have faith and trust in Him. To know and understand that he can deliver us through any situation.

Although, I'm sure it may have seemed and felt like an eternity to the people of the land of Egypt, who were praying unto God, but somehow they had faith that God can and will hear their cry. Their faith was mighty strong, because obviously they couldn't see God, but through their faith they could.

However, God was right there the whole entire time, working to hear and answer their prayers. In other words, working to answer what they were asking Him for.

It is very simple; it's all about trust with God. It's what God is looking for… to trust in Him and to believe in Him all of the time.

God's message to us is, when He doesn't answer our prayers instantly, it's not because He doesn't want to hear and see us, but it is because He wants us to build all of our trust and faith in Him. This is why God uses our situations to show his awesome power to us, so we can see that he is real, and he is totally awesome.

> Well my friends; do you want God to be totally
> awesome to you? Then you have to trust
> in Him. Our God is an awesome God!!!

God is calling all people to pray unto Him (those with a sincere heart) and he desires to talk to us through prayer. Prayer is to communicate with God. Jesus teaches us to pray often.

This shows that we want to have a true relationship with God, when we pray to Him.

From the old testament to the New Testament, you'll find people in the bible that were praying unto God. This teaches us that God loves for people to pray and talk to Him.

He is available to us all day and every day. God is ready to listen and answer each and every prayer that comes before Him. Especially, when it comes to children/kids. So, always remember God, and pray to Him often.

What a friend we have in Jesus!

Now that you know all of this, if someone would ever ask you the question, 'since God loves you so much, then why hasn't he answered your prayers yet?' you tell Him or her that God knows the right timing, and it's sure not yours, but on his timing, and his timing is the right timing.

When your prayer is answered by Him you will feel a big smile on your face and in your spirit.

It will be such a sweet feeling to your soul to let you know God does answer all your prayers.

In the Bible it says:

"*I cried unto the lord with my voice; with my voice unto the lord did I make my supplication. I poured out my complaint before Him; showed before Him my trouble.*"

-Psalms 142:1-2 (K.J.V)

CHAPTER FOUR

STAYING CONNECTED TO GOD AS YOU GROW

Kids, now we will be discussing how to stay connected with God as you grow into becoming an adult. As parents, we understand what it's like to be faced with peer-pressure. You must remember, we adults were kids too. Therefore, we understand most of the issues that you all must face.

If you're wondering why I said most issues, well, it's because you all are growing up so fast, it's so hard for us adults to keep up with the times, and for other adults, they may be a bit old-fashioned, that is to say, (stuck back in their past). But I'm sure even they understand most/some of the issues that you kids face as you're growing up.

This is why parents spend most of their time teaching those do's and don'ts. See, we parents have been taught by our parents as well, and so now we pass those teaching down to you. As you will later learn, those do's and don'ts will protect you and guide you safely through life.

Your parents know that you will be faced with making decisions based on those do's and don'ts, and that they may not be there to help you, so you'll have to make those decisions all by yourself.

Life does go on, and there will come a time when those rough and tough situations happen, and at those times you will have to choose between what your friends want you to do, and what your parents have taught you to do.

I'm pretty sure you're going to think, that if your parents were there it would be very easy for you to go ahead and say no to temptation, as your parents taught you to do.

The fact of the matter is, when we stay connected to God, it won't be as easy for us to make those wrong decisions. God knows none of us are perfect, but we can avoid those dumb and stupid choices just by listening to Him, and remembering what we were trained to do from our wonderfully guided parents. If you stay connected to God, you will be guided by His Awesome Holy Spirit.

And guess what? You won't have to wish or wonder that your parents were there with you, because God will let you know quickly the decisions that you should make to every situation.
(NOW ISN'T THAT AWESOME!)

This is why it's so very important for you to get familiar will God's voice, where you can recognize Him. Therefore, He can lead and guide you to that perfect decision.

I recall as a young kid, when my mother used to call me into the house when it was time to eat dinner. I could be blocks away from the house; the cars would be going up and down the street and I could still hear my mother's voice; it was so loud and clear.

Do you know why I was able to hear my mother's voice, so loud and clear? That's because I had to become so familiar with her voice.

In fact, you probably know what I mean because I'm sure that you can do the same thing with your parent's voice, hearing and recognizing it from far away. It's only because you have heard that voice so many times, and in so many ways that it's easy for you to identify.

Well, by the same token, God wants you to stay connected to Him, so that you know His voice, no matter where you are or how many people or kids are around. So no matter how far away you are, you will be able to identify the Voice of God, and recognize His words right away.

God's voice is your connection with Him, and He wants you to stay connected.

God already knows all the things that you are going to face as you grow up into an adult. He just wants to be a part of your decision making process, so that you will make those perfect choices.

God seeks to be a part of all our decisions that we make, so we can make a perfect and Godly choice.

We, as parents, only know most of the choices you as kids are going to make. But God knows every decision; if you dishonor your mother or father, He knows this as well.

For example, if you decide to use or sell drugs, break the law by stealing, or in any way at all, He knows. If you make a decision to dishonor your mother or father, He knows this as well. If you decide to use or sell drugs, break the law by stealing, or in any way at all, He knows. If you quit school, don't go to church, or stop reading your Bible, or forsake Him/God: HE ALREADY KNOWS!

Therefore, you need to make a good choice to stay connected to God as you grow, and strive to be obedient unto Him.

Whatever the case may be, God wants to be right there with you, guiding you to make the right and perfect choices as you stay connected to Him.

Phat – Krusher has given you a list of things to help you stay connected to God as you grow into young adults. This is what "The Phat – Krusher" calls **"The Connection of Communication,"** and I'll just list (7) of them for you:

THE PHAT – KRUSHER **"CONNECT TO CONNECT"** LIST

1. **Connect to Connect**: To God and the Bible. Schedule a specific time, 15 to 30 minutes with God a day.

2. **Connect to Connect**: To pray and talk unto God, day by day.

3. **Connect to Connect**: To being around kids your age and people that love God as much as you do.

4. **Connect to Connect**: To give thanks unto God for your protection, food, waking you up each day, his providence and His Awesome love for you.

5. **Connect to Connect**: To not ever be ashamed or embarrassed neither of God, nor of Jesus, or being around others that love and cherish God and Jesus as much as you do.

6. **Connect to Connect**: To ask God for his help as you get into difficult situations. To also allow God to be involved in your hurts, because He's truly the best at fixing people.

7. **Connect to Connect**: To the church, Gospel programs at church, be active in the church, Gospel TV Programs, Gospel Music, and spiritual materials.

Remember kids, if you want to show your friends who's really cool, then you just stay connected with the Awesome and cool God, and use this list to help you.

God leaves us many things, and ways to stay connected to Him. These things and ways demonstrate that He's there for us in every situation.

On the other hand, you may know of some people right now that make bad choices in their lives. And it's only because these kinds of people aren't familiar with God, nor His voice – That they aren't connected! If they were connected they wouldn't make those bad choices that put them in bad situations in the first place.

These kinds of people have never learned how to have a personal relationship with God, to learn why they make all of the bad and poor choices in their lives.

Neither God, nor your parents want you to make any bad decisions. And do you know why? It's because they love you so much.

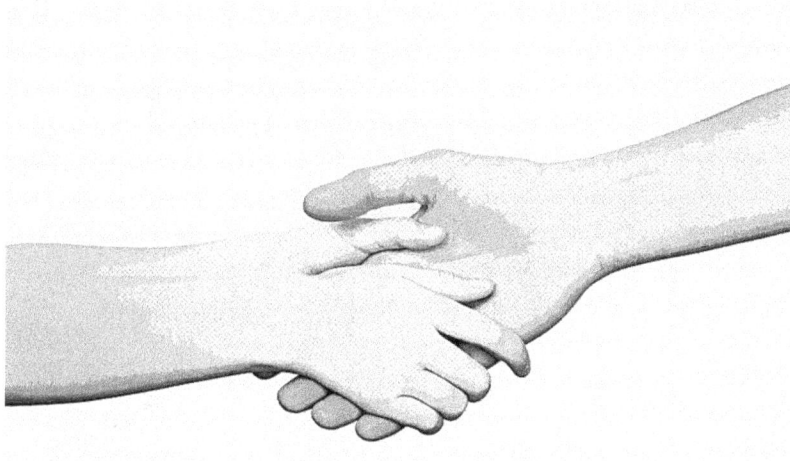

Remember! You were created for a greater purpose in this life.
You have the ability to be an awesome human being that God wants you to be, and you do this by honoring and respecting God. Having good morals, and being a decent person towards your parents and to other people in the world. Set your goals high towards God. He's there waiting to bless you with an abundance in this life and the next life.

"Stay connected to God... He loves you so much!"

CHAPTER FIVE

EATING THE RIGHT FOODS TO REMAIN HEALTHY

My friends! You have covered a lot of things in this book that are designed to help you have a healthy relationship with God and your parents. Now we'll deal with how you can have a healthy physical relationship as well.

For example, in order to keep something alive you must feed it or else it will fade and die. It must have nourishment/balance, just like the green grass that we all play, walk, and picnic on. If the grass doesn't have the right amount of water, minerals and sunlight, then it will start to fade, and die. All because it didn't have the right amount of balanced nourishment.

This happens to our physical bodies as well. We must nourish our bodies with the right foods or else we will soon start to fade away and die much sooner than we would have liked. And you know what? Our spiritual bodies desire the same thing, to be nourished in our LORD'S PRESENCE…

Do you want to know how we can do this? We do this by praying to God, or going to a church, listening to God's words while you are around other Christians. He loves to hear us sing the gospels to His Glory, or to read His book, the Bible. And He repays us by nourishing us in HIS GLORIOUS PRESENCE.

So, by meeting all the right requirements to your physical and spiritual bodies, you will be a healthy and balanced person. This is what God and your parents want for you!

Well, by the same token this also applies to the physical body that you now live in, and it's what you call the physical side.

Now we will be discussing eating the right kinds of foods and also the things that you need to develop that healthy – physically fit body. Making better, healthier choices can make your life last longer. On the other hand, making poor health choices can increase your risk of having bad health, which can lead to an early death. Bad health choices can also cause you to become overweight or obese.

Did you know that a 2009 survey listed Miami, Florida as one of the highest cities when it came to obesity? There are over two-million children under the age of six who are obese in this world, right now. Can you believe it? This is a problem kids, and it needs to be solved. It can be – by finding better ways to eat, and by being more physically active through exercise, sports, and games.

African - Americans make a large majority of the obese people in the United States? Seventy-five percent of African American women are obese and 65% of the men. And it doesn't stop there; the kids are represented as well, with the girls at 25% and the boys at 18%!

Did you know that African Americans are twice more likely to suffer a heart attack or stroke than any other race of people?

It's time for all people around the globe to make a stand, and that time is now! Your health is a serious matter to God, and it should be to us as well.

God wants you to live a long and healthy life, so you will be able to enjoy every blessing that He has coming your way.

Spending all of your life going to the hospital, seeing doctors or worrying about a bunch of medical bills isn't what God intended for us to do, especially in these times. Besides, who can afford those medical bills? So you youngsters must make better choices on how you eat, if you want to see tomorrow and a better you. You can enjoy seeing years of a better you, by moving towards a change of being health conscious (AWARE!).

This is what I call wellness; a state of being in good health, and enjoying life. Being physically active can have a positive impact in the later years of your life.

Also, eating the right foods can make you healthier, and can help you to live longer. That is why it's important for you to get rid of those junk foods, or to at least cut back on them. Unhealthy foods, such as: sugary cereals, cookies, candy, soda pops, potato chips, greasy fried foods, processed meats – packaged hot dogs, bologna meats, and of course those red meats, are all foods that I call "Ugly junk-foods."

Eating sugary foods can increase your chance of having bad teeth. It can also lead to bad health problems such as diabetes and heart disease. If you want a healthier lifestyle, and to live longer, you must start eating better foods… foods such as: fresh fruits, vegetables, beans, nuts, brown rice, oatmeal, and whole-grain products that are low in sodium. Also, low-fat dairy products such as yogurt or cottage cheese. And when you eat meat products try to find meats that are leaner cuts (that have had fat removed) such as round roast or poultry, plus when you eat chicken try not to eat fried chicken or at least, don't eat the skin. Try to drink plenty of water… you need 6 to 8 cups of water a day, and no kids, this doesn't include sodas.

You must also learn how to put video games aside… I know, I know… You must also learn to put aside the DVDs, TV programs, and other electronic devices, so that you can become more active, and spend less time in your rooms and more time on your feet. Go visit your friends next-door instead of just 'texting' them, play a real game of soccer, or basketball instead of using a gaming device. In fact, why not take up a sport, or recreational activity such as: riding your bike, or swimming at the local YMCA. The point is that it doesn't really matter what you choose to do, it's just that you do it! And the great thing is that this will help keep your heart working at its best, and keep your weight under control. The Phat – Krusher is positively trying to help you kids to not fall into the overweight category. Don't be a statistic kids. Let's learn how to get fit!!!

PREVENTION IS ALWAYS BETTER THAN A CURE!

If you want to live a healthy, long, physical life, so that you can take care of your parents when they need you, then you must stay in good health or else your parents will be taking care of you instead. God has a good life planned for you, but you have to eat the right foods in order to receive or obtain it, so you can enjoy it (Life).

TO PARENTS:

Therefore, parents, it's your time to start buying healthier foods for the nourishment of your children. How can your child learn to eat healthy when 'junk foods' are constantly being bought for them?

By taking the steps to a healthier life, you and your children will be happier and healthier in the long run.

If you want to lose weight then you must start making healthier choices. I have another book entitled "Phat - Krusher" and if you want the fat to just melt away, I highly suggest my book for you. God only desires the best possible life for you and your family. And for the people that decided to be obedient unto Him, He gives them the best and more.

Love your children, and keep them healthy; spiritually and physically. May God bless you all, and may all your children's dreams comes true and yours as well.

LET'S STAY HEALTHY!

Well, by now you should know that I like to use the number seven, which is known as God's "perfection" and "completion" number. Therefore, I'm only going to establish seven questions and answers that kids may want to ask, or are curious about.

1. Who made or created God?

God was not made or created; He just is who He is. The Bible reads that *"God is the Alpha, and the Omega, the beginning and the ending, said the Lord, which is and which was and which is to come, the Almighty."*

– Revelations 1:8

2. Who is Jesus?

The Bible says that *"Jesus is the son of God, God sent Him into the world that we might live through Him, so that we can be with God. For God sent not His Son, into the world to condemn the world; but that the world through Him might be saved."*

– John 3:16-17

3. Is Jesus God?

This is why it's so important that you get familiar with God and Jesus for yourself, so it can be revealed unto you or uncovered unto you.

The Bible says: *"A man called Simon Peter said unto Jesus, some say that you are John the Baptist. Some say you are Elijah, and some others say you are Jeremiah, or one of the prophets. And Jesus said unto Him, but who do you say I am? And Simon Peter answered and said unto Jesus, you're the Christ, and the Son of the Loving God. And Jesus answered and said unto Peter, blessed are you, Simon Bar-Jona for flesh and blood had not revealed it to you, but my Father which is in heaven."*

– Matthew 16:14-17

The Bible says: *"… the Jews unto Him, you are not fifty years old and you have seen Abraham? Jesus said unto them, "Verily, verily, I say unto you, before Abraham was I."*

– John 8:57-58

Also, in the Book of James, *"If any of you lack wisdom or understanding let Him or her ask of God, and He will give it to all people freely, and not (expose), and it shall be given to them."*

– James 1:5

So ask God and He will show you who Jesus really is. He will reveal it to you.

4. Why is the number seven God's 'perfection' and 'completion' number?

"It took God six days to make the world and create us. He rested on the Seventh day."

— Genesis 1:1-31, 2:1-3

"It took seven priests to march or encompass around the wall of Jericho, seven times for the wall to come falling down."

— Joshua 6:4

"God said a just person will fall seven times and rise up again."

— Proverbs 24:16

"It took Elijah's servant seven times to look for rain."

— 1 Kings 18:43

This is why I love to use the number seven, because it's God's 'perfection' and 'completion' number.

5. Why do we all have to die at some point?

God wants us to live that perfect life, just like Him. But in order to do that we must die a physical death, therefore, we can get out of this body, because it's no good unto God, it's always doing bad towards God. So it must die, and then God can give us a new and glorious body, and it will be perfect, just the way God intended it to be. However, at this time our spirit can be perfect to love God and others, just like God's love is perfect towards us. The Bible says, "Be therefore perfect (perfect in your love) even as your Father which is in Heaven is Perfect."

In the Bible, Jesus says, *"Let not your heart be troubled: you believe in God, believe also in Me. In my Father's House are many mansions: if it were not so, I would have not told you. I go to prepare a place for you. And if I go and prepare a place for you, I will come again, and receive you unto Myself, that where I am, there you may be also."*

-Matthew 5:48 and John 14:1-3

6. Why do I have to go to Church?

You don't have to go to Church. However, it's very good that you do go to Church, so you can hear the Word of God, and meet the people that share your same faith, and loves Jesus and God as much as you. Therefore, you can grow up very strong in the Lord, by eating the right spiritual foods. Going to church will also help you get familiar with your spiritual brothers and sisters that share your love of our Lord Jesus Christ and His Father God. So, if your current age group of peers don't know about and love our Lord as much as you, well, you surely can hang around the people that you've met, or will meet at church. Now, I'm sure that you'll miss a few Sundays, your human after all, but please try to not miss too many out of the month. Please note: Miss them because you have to, not because you want to.

Lastly, it's my responsibility to ask the parents and the children: Have you settled to trust Jesus Christ as your personal Savior?

For that matter, do you yearn to have a personal relationship with the one who created you and loves you, no matter what?

If this is your case, tell Him in your own words, or use this sample prayer:

"Dear heavenly Father, I acknowledge that I'm wrong, and you are always right. For I am a sinner in need of your forgiveness. I believe fully, that Jesus paid the penalty for all my sins by dying on the cross at Calvary, and that He rose from the dead. Thank you for that, and for your grace to save me even though I am so un-deserving. Please, Father, show me how to start living for you… Amen."

If you have made such a decision to receive Jesus Christ into your life, The Phat- Krusher encourages you to prayer-fully seek a local, mature church, where you can grow as a new Christian, by the clear teaching of God's word (The Bible)."

Once again, I am so humble for the parents and the children for beckoning me into your home for an enjoyable entertainment of your physical life and the next life that awaits us all.

I thank you all!

ABOUT THE AUTHOR

Al Wordly is the prestigious author of Spiritual & Physical Fitness, Ten Years a Successful Marriage, and many more books.

In his free time, he enjoys conversing with family and friends and making others feel special.

He is living proof of staying spiritually and physically fit in order to maintain a healthy lifestyle.

Currently, he resides in Miami, Florida continuing to strive to the Top.

PHAT·KRUSHER

SQUISH FAT LIKE A JELLY BEAN

www.ingramcontent.com/pod-product-compliance
Lightning Source LLC
Chambersburg PA
CBHW080938040426
42443CB00015B/3463